Sabhya & Saachi Series

Authored and Conceptualized by:
Ms. Dimple Dang

Edited by:
Dr. Amit Dang

Illustrated and Designed by:
Mr. Tridib Ghosh (Team Chlorosynth)

Instagram: @sabhya.saachi

Note to parents

Dear Parents,

Thank you for choosing **"Screen Time vs Play Time: A Balancing Act"** for your child.

This book aims to turn screen time into an engaging learning experience and make playtime equally exciting, all while fostering balance and family bonds.

Here are some quick tips for balancing screen use and playtime to support healthier habits.

- **Balanced lifestyle:** Foster a balanced lifestyle as a family by participating in activities together. Prioritize quality time through reading, outdoor adventures, and limited screen time.
- **Exploration and learning:** Encourage your child's curiosity and creativity. Explore the wonders of the natural world and engage them in "learning on the go" experiences.
- **Tech free zones:** Create designated areas in your home free from screens. Promote meaningful face-to-face interactions and quality family time. These activities not only entertain but also create stronger family bonds.
- **Role modelling:** Lead by example. Engage in non-screen activities alongside your child to influence their behaviours and preferences positively. Create lasting memories through shared family time, where laughter and togetherness are the key ingredients.
- **Unplug for playtime:** Embrace the joy of play. Encourage your child to unplug from screens and immerse themselves in imaginative and active playtime.

We hope that **"Screen Time Vs Play Time: A Balancing Act"** becomes a valuable addition to your family's journey. Together, you can find the perfect harmony between screens and real-world adventures, fostering a loving, healthy, and joyful family life.

Sincerely,
Dimple Dang

Saachi and Sabhya are a brother-sister duo who love to explore, play, and learn together. Saachi is the older sibling and she's always ready for adventure with her boundless energy and clever wit. Sabhya is the younger one, growing up fast and enthusiastic about discovering new things. Together, they are two peas in a pod, a double dose of adventure, and twice the fun!

© Dimple Dang 2024

All rights reserved

All rights reserved by author. No part of this publication may be reproduced, stored in a retrieval system or transmitted in any form or by any means, electronic, mechanical, photocopying, recording or otherwise, without the prior permission of the author. Although every precaution has been taken to verify the accuracy of the information contained herein, the author and publisher assume no responsibility for any errors or omissions. No liability is assumed for damages that may result from the use of information contained within.

First Published in **2024**

ISBN: 978-93-6261-967-9

Authored and Conceptualized by:
Ms. Dimple Dang

Edited by:
Dr. Amit Dang

Illustrated and Designed by:
Mr. Tridib Ghosh (Team Chlorosynth)

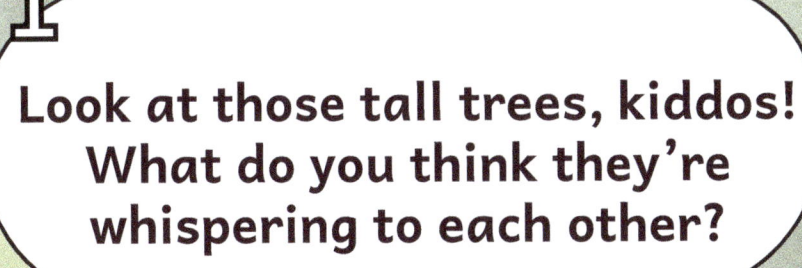

1. Look at those tall trees, kiddos! What do you think they're whispering to each other?

2. Oh, look, a fluffy cloud! It's playing hide-and-seek with the sun!

Family Fun: Splash and Swim Time

1. Look, Mom, I can swim like a fish now!

2. That's fantastic, Saachi! Swimming is not only fun but also an important life skill.

Moral of the story

While screens can be fun and informative, it's important not to forget the joy, creativity, and social connections that come from playing and exploring the real world. By finding the right balance between screen time and playtime, we can lead fulfilling lives, nurture our physical and mental well-being, and build meaningful relationships.

Impact of Screen Time Vs Play Time

Screen Time	Play Time
Inactive	Active
Solitary	Social
Lethargic	Learner

Screen Time	Play Time
Grumpy 	**Joyful** 
Strained 	**Relaxed** 
Restless 	**Soundsleep** 

These are the everyday moments at our home..

www.ingramcontent.com/pod-product-compliance
Lightning Source LLC
LaVergne TN
LVHW070602070526
838199LV00011B/460